NO LONGER BOUND

INSPIRATIONAL POEMS FROM THE WISDOM OF GOD

DEDRA JOHNSON

No Longer Bound

This book is written to provide information and motivation to readers. Its purpose is not to render any type of psychological, legal, or professional advice of any kind. The content is the sole opinion and expression of the author, and not necessarily that of the publisher.

Copyright © 2021 by Dedra Johnson.

All rights reserved. No part of this book may be reproduced, transmitted, or distributed in any form by any means, including, but not limited to, recording, photocopying, or taking screenshots of parts of the book, without prior written permission from the author or the publisher. Brief quotations for noncommercial purposes, such as book reviews, permitted by Fair Use of the U.S. Copyright Law, are allowed without written permissions, as long as such quotations do not cause damage to the book's commercial value. For permissions, write to the publisher, whose address is stated below.

Printed in the United States of America.

ISBN   978-1-955363-04-4   (Paperback)
ISBN   978-1-955363-05-1   (Digital)

Lettra Press books may be ordered through booksellers or by contacting:

Lettra Press LLC
30 N Gould St. Suite 4753
Sheridan, WY 82801
1 307-200-3414 | info@lettrapress.com
www.lettrapress.com

CONTENTS

Dedication v
Preface vii
Acknowledgements ix
Introduction xi

1. Withholding the Fruit of the Spirit................................ 1
2. Fit for the Fight 4
3. The Guilt of the Adulteress 7
4. Confronting the Enemy 10
5. JEZEBEL, YOU MUST GO! 13
6. How Great the Temptation 16
7. Where are You, Man of God? 19
8. Growing in Perfection... 22
9. Take Your Hands off My Inheritance 25
10. Wisdom to Face My Demons 28
11. Graced 31
12. Who Am I?.. 34
13. The Challenge of Maturing in God............................. 37
14. Do You have the Character? 40
15. Christ, Your Bride Awaits 43
16. When the Inner Man Cries Out 46
17. The Weight of Forgiving Wrong................................. 49
18. The Outlook of Restoration 52
19. I Am Ruth 55
20. How Long Will You Reject Me? 58

Appendix 1: The Practice Guide 61
Appendix 2: The Deliverance Prayer 65
Appendix 3: Confessions of Gratitude 69
Appendix 4: Three-Part Being of Man 73
Appendix 5: The Process to Destiny.................................. 75

DEDICATION

This book is dedicated to my children, Demara and Carwyn.

PREFACE

No Longer Bound is not just a book of poems but also a practical reference guide one can use to get a breakthrough from the problems he or she may face while living in this world. I asked God to make me whole again. How was He going to do it? I did not know for sure. I knew I did my own thing in the beginning with the hope of living out my dreams, which never happened up to this point. Can you remember how Danny Glover slapped Whoopi Goldberg constantly in the movie The Color Purple? No matter what Miss Celie did to help make his life better, it was never good enough for Mister Albert. That was exactly the way I felt-feeling like there was no possibility of getting back up. Satan threw some low blows, using my weaknesses against me and not caring who he used to wreak havoc in my life. Only God could help me out of the pit that I was in. I almost lost my mind, but writing was like a medicine to my brain. The lightbulb came on in my head without me having to pull the string. I was able to be creative with my thoughts by writing poetry. The last time I wrote anything was over ten years ago to get my master's degree.

I thank God for giving me the strength to write this book while going through adversity. He was stretching me and preparing me to be someone great. After learning how Satan works, I knew I had fallen amongst thieves. My goal is to take back everything that belongs to me. "And I will restore to you the years that the locust hath eaten, the cankerworm, and the caterpillar, and the palmerworm, my great army which I sent among you" (Joel 2:25). I made up my mind to trust God through the process. No matter who gives advice, always weigh it according to the Word of God. Each topic of the poem was dropped in my spirit and I searched the scriptures to give me an outline of how to write them. The bottom line was that I had issues, and I needed answers. God knows what is best, so I turned to Him. He guided me every step of the way.

I got the chance to experience what the disciples experienced as they were inspired by God to write the scriptures of the Bible. I was inspired to write simple poems about my life, integrating the Word of God to bring deliverance to you in the name of Jesus…something simple, but powerful. According to 1 Corinthians 1:27, "God chose the foolish and weak things of the world to confound the wise and the mighty things." Since I am able to talk, I will use my mouth to call the promises of God into existence. "Death and life are in the power of the tongue: and they that love it shall eat the fruit thereof" (Prov. 18:21). I will speak life over a dead situation. I will do my part and let God do His part whether what I say manifests now or later. Besides, it is time for revival and for the kingdom of God to be at hand in miracles, signs, and wonders.

ACKNOWLEDGEMENTS

I would like to thank God first and foremost for answering my prayer for wholeness.

Special thanks to my family, especially my parents, who endured the process of my journey.

I also want to give honor to my former Pastor Creflo Dollar and his wife, Taffi Dollar for helping me to understand grace.

INTRODUCTION

*I will instruct you and teach you in
the way which you should go;
I will counsel you with My eye upon you.*
Psalms 32:8 (KJV)

I survived several obstacles thanks to my awesome teacher, the Holy Spirit. The lessons learned from my struggles increased as I gained sight and dependence on God to proceed forward. It did not take attending school or seminars to learn such life-changing principles. The world consists of people with different personalities and different mindsets that produce different behaviors. You cannot avoid people, unless you isolate yourself from them. At first, depression had me bound-so bound that I hid behind closed doors where I did not want to get out of my bed. I did not want to be bothered by anyone. Did you know deliverance from people was essential in progression? I was disturbed by their speech and their actions. Literally, I was drained from the negative energy. I did not know what to do. It is true to be careful of the company that you keep, especially in your inner circle. I sought help from every source, but the right source was God. When I realized that I could not control people through manipulation, I was liberated by changing my response to every experience.

I learned my identity in Christ and began to use the spiritual authority He gave to me. I even let fear contaminate my faith in God. I quoted 2 Timothy 1:7 so much that I stopped believing it was true because I knew what I saw and how I felt. I studied that scripture to correct my mistakes. I did not fear that God would not heal me because if I could talk to a headache and the pain left, I could believe in something greater. I knew there was power in the name of Jesus. I knew God loved me, and healing was part of His will. My mind was the only thing left to analyze. There was absolutely a war going on in my mind spiritually (life) and carnally (death). Sometimes, I would overthink a situation, especially after hearing a person's testimony. My mind would shift all over the place when I should have been steadfast in my faith, not moved by what others said or what they did.

I looked at the woman with the issue of blood for twelve years in the Bible. In her mind, she knew she would be healed once she touched Jesus's garment. Immediately, she was made whole because of her faith. I had to renew my mind and face my fears to free myself from bondage in order to reach my destiny. "But without faith it is impossible to please Him, for he who comes to God must believe that He is, and that He is a rewarder of those who diligently seek Him" (Heb. 11:6 NKJV). After hearing a sermon on faith, I grabbed what I needed to proceed forward in my healing instead of allowing that word to fall by the wayside, choked, or stolen from me. I believed God's report rather than man's report.

I can recall when I was on my way to work one morning when I felt my strength leaving me. Everything around me turned gray. I began gasping for breath. I pushed the button for my emergency lights and drifted off the road into a driveway. I did not know fainting was common during pregnancy; my baby was sitting in the wrong position. The only thing I could think of was by your stripes Lord, I am healed. I said this repetitively until my strength came back to me. Because I was crying out to God, He came to my rescue by giving me His strength to go on to work. Yes, I could have gone back home, but I did my duty for that day. My boss told me that God had His angels watching over me. I thank God for His protection.

I was a challenger and a risk-taker who knew how to play it safe. I would try anything for instant pleasure and acceptance. I became a totally different person if dared in a negative or positive manner. Am I mysterious? Yes, I am. I am grateful for songs of deliverance, sermons, and the scriptures to get me back on the right trajectory after I missed the mark. I witnessed two elders put down their cane and walker, several who were healed, and others who experienced financial breakthroughs after I spoke the Word with faith to them. I know what God can do. We pray the Lord's Prayer, asking God to let His kingdom come on earth as it is in heaven. Do we really believe the actual words we pray? I want to experience the supernatural power of our true living God on earth, not kundalini, chi, or any other kind of magic. God is greater! My pastor at that time used the phrases, "You have to work the Word" and "if you believe right, then you can live right." I will follow those commands just to see manifestation.

How long was the question I would ask myself or what is blocking me…generational or word curses, evil altars, etc. I did not know. I prayed, I fasted, deprived myself of a lot of things to grow spiritually… working out my own salvation. I stopped going to church because of what I was experiencing in the atmosphere. I was doing church virtually instead. I thought I would be safe and better off at receiving from the Lord, but I was feeling a strange presence coming through the screen of my laptop and cellphone. Then, I would sometimes feel a sting, a dart, a stab, or illness in my body. I was under spiritual attack. I would ask questions from those who I thought had knowledge of the subject. I didn't get anywhere with that. I didn't want to perish because of lack of knowledge. Since this was spiritual and there was no distance in the spirit realm, it was time for one on one with God for sure. Enough of being on the surface, it was time to go deeper. Yes, I went there, but some things you have to let go of and just let God handle it. Since my attitude will determine my altitude, I am humble, thankful, under God's armor, gracious, and forever praising God to ease my anxiety and frustration.

Will you trust God? Will you consider His Word? As I said before, it took the scriptures to bring life back to my wretched soul. The best wisdom you can obtain is from God through His Word. Proverbs 4:7 states, "Wisdom is the principal thing; therefore get wisdom: and with all thy getting get understanding." I was baffled to reap the negative benefits of others' advice. The minute I submitted to God, I got my breakthrough by waiting patiently. It took longer than I expected, but my timing was not God's timing. Letting go of the lesser things of my flesh made it easier to walk in the Holy Spirit. I pursued the things of the Spirit because I had a hunger for God to demonstrate His glory in our lives. I was determined to let go of associates, jobs, and habits to see results. I cut off everything that did not contribute to my growth. I was adamant to follow that voice saying, "Don't throw out the baby with the bathwater." I will not deceive you. When I made God top priority in my life, all *hell* broke loose. I tried to keep my focus as being a light in a dark place, the salt of the earth, and on fire for God.

I was sidetracked, distracted, hindered, or whatever you want to call it. Almost every negative emotion resided in me deeply. I was angry and bitter on a daily basis where hatred developed in my heart. Can you imagine me arguing with a person until I had the last word? If you struck my nerve, you should expect a hit upside the head, in the mouth, or somewhere in the upper body. I knew retaliation or character assassination was wrong. I destroyed several relationships because of my words and actions. I knew being in this state would cause my health to decline, so I had to do something about it. I did not turn to a doctor for medical treatment. I prayed to God, read His Word, sought spiritual counseling, and just *believed*.

I looked up scriptures on anger and bitterness like James 1:19, Ephesians 4:26, and Proverbs 15:1. The scriptures that I declared the most was Ephesians 4:31-32, "Let all bitterness, and wrath, and anger, and clamor, and evil speaking, be put away from you, with all malice: And be ye kind one to another, tenderhearted, forgiving one another, even as God for Christ's sake hath forgiven you." As you can see, the scriptures identified what I was going through and gave me solutions to my problems. I applied the other scriptures since they were practical in knowing how to interact with people. The best practice is to always start at home.

One thing I can say, the Word spoken aloud will change the atmosphere around you when you are in alignment with God. If you want peace, ask God for it. Are you willing to let go of greed, bitterness, anger, self-centeredness, jealousy, hatred, lust, addiction, or whatever is hindering you from being a mature Christian? The choice is yours to heal from your mistakes and insecurities. Never let them destroy you. Speaking of maturity, recently, I had to deal with the spirits of python, religion, Jezebel, and witchcraft all at the same time. Now, you know I had to equip myself quickly in spiritual warfare because

I realized that Satan wanted me dead. He was not playing either, so I put on God's armor because this was my evil day; I needed Him to fight for me. God will give you that same boldness He gave me to fight your battles. Effective spiritual warfare helps, but that is another discussion for another time. Eventually, healing will come when you humble yourself under the mighty hand of God, reveal your secrets, and deal with your issues.

God has been there for me the whole time, from my childhood until now. I was just unaware of it. The same way God was with Joshua, He is with me everywhere I go. I am thankful to be alive. I have fallen asleep and blanked out while driving, fainted from having low blood glucose levels, had low hemoglobin readings (6.4 being the lowest), suffered from depression and rejection from failed relationships, and other complications. Yet God kept me. I embedded Isaiah 53:5 personally in my spirit. I am a walking testimony or a wonder with feet because God has allowed me to survive everything Satan has thrown at me, although some were self-inflicted. I can go on and on about how God has proven Himself to me. He is my strength in my weakness. Even my desires changed to His desires. I can do nothing without Him. I can admit that I should get out of His way from time to time.

God moved in my situations so miraculously that I have to praise Him. I had planned my future. I wanted two children, a boy and a girl. My daughter was born first. Then, I started having complications that put me at high risk for a second pregnancy. I still wanted my boy. I had all kinds of tests done to see what was really going on with me. I was disappointed in God because He allowed me to rejoice in knowing I could conceive a child after having the hysterosalpingogram (HSG) procedure done. I left the hospital thinking I could not have a baby ever again based on what I saw on the screen with my own eyes, dye trapped inside of my blocked fallopian tubes. The nurse called me later that day to tell me that the pictures taken actually showed the opposite. Weeks had passed and guess what? I was pregnant, but death knocked on the door of my womb when I was 17 weeks. I was having a miscarriage and did not know it. The pain was so excruciating that it had me on my hands and knees where I could barely sit or sleep.

As I laid in the hospital bed, I looked at my spouse overwhelmed with grief. I turned my head from him to the window. It was at that very moment when God gave me peace about my loss. Sometimes, we do not understand how God orchestrates things to happen, but He made it possible for me to encourage one of my nurses. She wondered how I could encourage her after what had just happened to me. I told her it was nobody but the Lord. The doctor sent me home with pain killers that did not work, so I had to get a prescription for something stronger just to go asleep. I was grateful to receive the results I was looking for, but I did not want to be bed bound. I questioned God because I was standing on His promise.

My exact words were, "God, You said in Your Word that by Jesus's stripes I am healed, so why should I have to take this medicine for my healing? Pain, go now in the name of Jesus." I got up out of my bed to do something I had never done, following the instructions given in a sermon I had previously heard. Even though I still was in pain, I started cleaning my home while speaking the promise out loud. As I cleaned, the pain left me gradually. Then, I realized the pain was gone. God showed up and showed out. I know He is a restorer and my strength because I have my son who is now 9 years old. I thought he was a goner too because my umbilical cord had wrapped around his neck. An emergency cesarean was called to save his life. Faith with expectation attached will bring forth manifestation.

My purpose is to win souls to Christ. I encourage you to have a personal relationship with Him. Christ will help you in the difficult times of your life. You deserve to be free from all strongholds. If you want heaven to be your eternal home, there are guidelines you have to follow. You must love, make Jesus your lord and savior, and be sealed with the Holy Spirit. There is no other way. If you love God, you will not want to do anything to displease Him. Your dreams can come true if you stay focused. Please declare in the atmosphere, "I can do all things through Christ who strengthens me" (Phil. 4:13). You will receive God's promises if you follow His commands. He will give you favor. He will give to His children who walk upright (Ps. 84:11). You cannot just do what you want to do. Have patience, courage, and strength in the Lord to overcome every adversity. "Cast not away therefore your confidence, which hath great recompense of reward" (Heb. 10:35).

Would you let the scriptures come alive in your inner being? The Holy Spirit wants to talk to you, but you must get quiet before Him. You will have distractions because Satan does not want you to be alone with God in prayer. My desire is to see the Body of Christ rise up and be who God created them to be. With the Holy Spirit on the inside of us, I believe prayer and the belief in God's Word are the vehicles that should be used for the church to take its rightful place in our society. We have heard various interpretations and revelations from men, why is this world still in the state that it is in when there is always a cry for change? We want the best things in life, but doubt that God will do what is best for us. Here is someone who knows everything, can see everything, and can be everywhere at the same time. Continually, we tend to have a problem submitting to Him. Trust is definitely the issue. We can be in and out of relationships like stray dogs going from house to house looking for food, but refuse to have a relationship with Jesus, the Son of God, who died for us. He will love us no matter what we do, but let me remind you that there are consequences for your actions. We are the sum total of what we are as well as where we are because of our decisions.

I can see why the Lord wants us to renew our minds with the Word. Do you want to try it? If so, I have included a practice guide to help you learn how to personalize the scriptures. (Please refer to Appendix 1). This exercise will also teach you how to pray the Word of God effectively. May God answer your prayer requests and bring deliverance unto you as you read this book. I am on a mission to influence one individual at a time with the help of the Lord. My feet may not touch the entrances of homes, but with your assistance, this book can.

WITHHOLDING THE FRUIT OF THE SPIRIT

*For the fruit of the Spirit is in all goodness
and righteousness and truth.*
Ephesians 5:9

Love, you are the bond of perfection.
No one can take you away.
You cover all of my wrongs, which makes me so strong.

Joy, you fill me beyond my imagination.
I rejoice while I wait for my freedom.
My trials remain, but with gladness, I will not complain.

Peace, you can bear me in silence.
Receive me beyond all your understanding,
Sit like a dove at rest from above.

Long-suffering, you block my path;
Great are the pains you make me endure.
Frustration and confusion want to drive me insane, yet God still reigns.

Faith, you are my hope that I cannot see,
Covered by my beliefs mixed with actions as my proof.
My now may deceive, but one day I will receive.

Gentleness, wisdom is what I pursue.
My destiny is to be great in humility.
Show me the way so I will not stray.

Goodness, you see the need for God to supply.
Purposely, I walk with the confidence of Jesus's finished works.
Safe regardless of present evil, which all comes from the devil.

Meekness, you utter not during abuse,
You caught me with your approach by surprise.
Correction is the goal to restore, so I will obey, not ignore.

Temperance, you hold my fist as I bite my lip.
You resist me upon every attempt,
Even make me weep and still whom my God keeps.

Holy Spirit, help me with these to activate,
To develop not just one, two, or three,
But all to bear your fruit, dressed for God in the perfect suit.

Prayer

Heavenly Father, thank You for being who You are in my life. Since it is better to walk in Your spirit rather than my flesh, please help me to do so. In Jesus's name, I pray. Amen.

PRACTICE: Replace the problem with God's promises by looking up the key phrase "Fruit of the Spirit" in the Bible and applying the best scriptures that pertain to your situation. I have provided some scriptures below that you can use. Meditate on the promises until they reside in your spirit. Confess them out loud every time the problem tries to resurface.

Example: Problem – Hate, Fear / Promise – Love, Faith

SCRIPTURES TO PONDER:

John 13:34 ~ A new commandment I give unto you, that ye love one another; as I have loved you, that ye also love one another.

Nehemiah 8:10 ~ For the joy of the Lord is your strength.

John 16:33 ~ These things I have spoken unto you, that in me ye might have peace. In the world ye shall have tribulation: but be of good cheer; I have overcome the world.

Hebrews 11:1 ~ Now faith is the substance of things hoped for, the evidence of things not seen.

Titus 3:2 ~ To speak evil of no man, to be no brawlers, but gentle, shewing all meekness unto all men.

Galatians 6:1 ~ Brethren, if a man is overtaken in any trespass, you who are spiritual restore such a one in a spirit of gentleness, considering yourself lest you also be tempted (NKJV).

YOUR THOUGHTS:

_____
_____
_____
_____
_____
_____
_____
_____
_____
_____

FIT FOR THE FIGHT

Put on the whole armor of God that ye may be able to stand against the wiles of the devil.
Ephesians 6:11

God, am I fit for this fight?
The battle is not mine but Yours.
What if I cast this care?
Do I still need to do spiritual warfare?

Where is my helmet of salvation?
I must convince lost souls,
Tell how Jesus died to set us free,
Make this like going on a shopping spree.

Where is my breastplate of righteousness?
Lord, please help me!
My flesh longs for pleasure in all of its senses,
Let my soul be as white as all the picket fences.

Where is my belt of truth?
I need to conquer all evil,
To eliminate being deceived with a lie,
When no one really wants to die.

Where is my shield of faith?
God, you are the author and the finisher of it.
Confusion knocks on the door of my mind,
Surrounded by the unbelief of those I do not want to leave behind.

Where is my sword of the Spirit?
Ready I am to slash the air declaring God's word.
It is His commands we must keep,
Going beyond no matter how deep.

Are my feet shod with the gospel of peace?
The desire to hate resides than to love my enemy.
I want to change what is wrong for what is right.
The people I must judge with God's sight.

You said vengeance is Yours and that You will repay.
Oh God, Your way is not my way,
And Your thoughts are not my thoughts.
With a price, I was still bought.

God, hide fear away from me in the battle,
Neither by might nor power but by Your spirit.
I can stand knowing I have the victory.
With You, I can change history.

Lord, please teach me how to submit to You and how to resist the devil in order for him to flee from me. You have already won the battle, so help me to stand in the midst of it until the end. In Your Son, Jesus's name I pray. Amen.

PRACTICE: Replace the problem with God's promises by looking up the key phrase "Armor of God" in the Bible and applying the best scriptures that pertain to your situation. I have provided some scriptures below that you can use. Meditate on the promises until they reside in your spirit. Confess them out loud every time the problem tries to resurface.

Example: Problem – Handling it yourself
/ Promise – God's vengeance

Dedra Johnson

SCRIPTURES TO PONDER:

Ephesians 6:10-18 ~ 10 Finally, my brethren, be strong in the Lord, and in the power of his might. 11 Put on the whole armor of God that ye may be able to stand against the wiles of the devil. 12 For we wrestle not against flesh and blood, but against principalities, against powers, against the rulers of the darkness of this world, against spiritual wickedness in high places. 13 Wherefore take unto you the whole armor of God that ye may be able to withstand in the evil day, and having done all, to stand. 14 Stand therefore, having your loins girt about with truth, and having on the breastplate of righteousness; 15 And your feet shod with the preparation of the gospel of peace; 16 Above all, taking the shield of faith, wherewith ye shall be able to quench all the fiery darts of the wicked. 17 And take the helmet of salvation, and the sword of the Spirit, which is the word of God: 18 Praying always with all prayer and supplication in the Spirit, and watching thereunto with all perseverance and supplication for all saints.

1 Thessalonians 5:15 ~ See that none render evil for evil unto any man; but ever follow that which is good, both among yourselves, and to all men.

Romans 12:19 ~ Do not take revenge, my dear friends, but leave room for God's wrath, for it is written: "It is mine to avenge; I will repay," says the Lord (NIV).

YOUR THOUGHTS:

_____
_____
_____
_____
_____
_____
_____
_____
_____
_____

THE GUILT OF THE ADULTERESS

Whoever commits adultery with a woman lacks understanding;
He who does so destroys his own soul.
Proverbs 6:32 (NKJV)

One look, then another was all it took,
We both disobeyed the Good Book.
Against our bodies, we have transgressed,
Not calculating the hours we may be in distress.

Never thought I would play the card of a fool,
For something where I could not keep my cool.
What was done in the dark has been revealed,
For a bed defiled will take time to be healed.

With a heart so broken it may never be mended,
Afraid to be open because of what you hid and so pretended.
My focus broke and was interrupted by temptation,
Blinded by your constant penetration.

My life was robbed and crushed before everyone's eyes,
Half committed to a lifestyle I must say "goodbye".
Took by the bombshell of your lust nothing like God's love,
To escape the persecution of others then be judged from above.

Bound with chains around my neck, hands, and feet,
My thoughts so wild like I am every man's meat.

Each I must cast down so they won't manifest,
Regardless, I wait in patience for what is best.

Satan thought he had me, using his tricks to get me to sin,
The ditch people dug for me was their own reaped bin.
No weapon formed against me shall prosper,
Not even evil visiting me in the image of Casper.

For vengeance is not mine,
Justice will come in its time.
Thank you, Lord, for not taking the score.
I will go my way and sin no more.

Grateful for mercy in giving me a second chance,
Jesus, You covered me with the blood you shed in advance.
Great is the scarlet letter, but sufficient is your grace,
Glad I will be when I see your face.

Prayer

Lord, help me to keep my eyes on You. Let me desire to be a hearer and doer of Your Word. From now on, please prepare my heart to do Your will. In Jesus's name, I pray. Amen.

PRACTICE: Replace the problem with God's promises by looking up the keyword "adultery" in the Bible and applying the best scriptures that pertain to your situation. I have provided some scriptures below that you can use. Meditate on the promises until they reside in your spirit. Confess them out loud every time the problem tries to resurface.

Example: Problem – Adultery / Promise – Marriage

SCRIPTURES TO PONDER:

Hebrews 13:4 ~ Marriage is honorable in all, and the bed undefiled: but whoremongers and adulterers God will judge.

Matthew 19:9 ~ And I say to you, whoever divorces his wife, except for sexual immorality, and marries another, commits adultery; and whoever marries her who is divorced commits adultery (NKJV).

1 Corinthians 10:13 ~ There hath no temptation taken you but such as is common to man: but God is faithful, who will not suffer you to be tempted above that ye are able; but will with the temptation also make a way to escape, that ye may be able to bear it.

Romans 7:3 ~ So then if, while her husband lives, she marries another man, she will be called an adulteress; but if her husband dies, she is free from that law, so that she is no adulteress, though she has married another man (NKJV).

2 Corinthians 12:9 ~ And he said unto me, My grace is sufficient for thee: for my strength is made perfect in weakness. Most gladly therefore will I rather glory in my infirmities, that the power of Christ may rest upon me.

Isaiah 54:17 ~ No weapon formed against you shall prosper, and every tongue which rises against you in judgment you shall condemn. This is the heritage of the servants of the Lord, and their righteousness is of me, says the Lord (NKJV).

YOUR THOUGHTS:

_____
_____
_____
_____
_____
_____

CONFRONTING THE ENEMY

But love your enemies, do good, and lend,
hoping for nothing in return;
and your reward will be great, and
you will be sons of the Most High.
For He is kind to the unthankful and evil.
                    Luke 6:35 (NKJV)

Against me was the evil you thought,
Without knowing you were going to get caught.
Setting your own trap that bared your name,
Blind I was when framed but not the one to blame.

The enemy whom I fed had no clue,
Jesus would come to my rescue.
Wholeheartedly, I trust in Him and the heavenly cast.
I am confident that my troubles will not last.

I must forgive to free myself and acquire what is due.
I tried to warn you, even have compassion for you.
I won't boast because judgment is served,
But you got what you deserved.

God's command is to love, bless, and pray.
My mind and emotions are about to cause me to go astray.
Oh, God, it is you I must obey.
You will fight my opponent on any given day.

In ignorance, you chose lust over love for me.
Burning with fire and brimstone is what your end will be.
Hopefully, conviction will lead you to repentance.
Heaven you will not see without God's mercy and acceptance.

Deception canceled out everything that could bring merit.
Lust has caused this war between my flesh and spirit,
The confirmation that you are of your father, the devil.
I should have expected greater mischief with the new level.

Discouraged and afraid I will not be.
I know where my strength comes from when I am weak.
In peace, you, my enemy must bow and be at ease,
For with me, God is pleased.

Prayer

**Oh Lord, my God, help me to love my enemies as You have loved me. Help us to get along in peace and harmony even when we are faced with difficulties. In Jesus's name, I pray.
Amen.**

PRACTICE: Replace the problem with God's promises by looking up the keywords "enemy" or "friend" in the Bible and applying the best scriptures that pertain to your situation. I have provided some scriptures below that you can use. Meditate on the promises until they reside in your spirit. Confess them out loud every time the problem tries to resurface.

   Example: Problem – Enemy / Promise – Friend

Dedra Johnson

SCRIPTURES TO PONDER:

Luke 6:27-28 ~ 27 But I say unto you which hear, Love your enemies, do good to them which hate you, 28 Bless them that curse you, and pray for them which despitefully use you.

Proverbs 27:17 ~ As iron sharpens iron, so a man sharpens the countenance of his friend (NKJV).

Proverbs 16:7 ~ When a man's ways please the Lord, he maketh even his enemies to be at peace with him.

Psalms 37:1 ~ Fret not thyself because of evildoers, neither be thou envious against the workers of iniquity.

2 Corinthians 12:10 ~ Therefore I take pleasure in infirmities, in reproaches, in necessities, in persecutions, in distresses for Christ's sake: for when I am weak, then am I strong.

Galatians 6:7 ~ Be not deceived; God is not mocked: for whatsoever a man soweth, that shall he also reap.

Proverbs 18:24 ~ A man that hath friends must shew himself friendly: and there is a friend that sticketh closer than a brother.

YOUR THOUGHTS:

_____
_____
_____
_____
_____
_____
_____

JEZEBEL, YOU MUST GO!

*Nevertheless I have a few things against you, because
you allow that woman Jezebel,
Who calls herself a prophetess, to teach and seduce my
servants to commit sexual immorality,
And eat things sacrificed to idols.*
Revelation 2:20 (NKJV)

A faith so strong how could anyone go wrong,
For the love you share causes everyone to stare.
You set the table with food in reserve for the idols you serve,
And use words to seduce the people you will reduce.

A face made up to lure knowing your motives were impure,
Harm is what one gets for refusing to submit; why won't you admit?
You persist like this world and its lusts you could not resist.
The lack of trust is my issue when you plot and get others to pursue.

Let not your character be like Jezebel, Ahab's wife,
So wicked and manipulative as she stirred up strife.
It was Baal they worshipped as their god,
Distributed her witchcraft and filthiness abroad.

She hated God's prophets as she obtained wealth,
Pushed from the window of her bedroom to her death.
She was trampled by horses and eaten by dogs.
Her blood they licked up like the slop for hogs.

Perverse is your dominion from the dark as you hide behind religion.
Your actions were overlooked, but no more without rebuke.
Now you must repent before your judgment is sent;
Avoid your bed of sickness and your kids' death so others will not witness.

A great change is required of you and any who sleep with you too.
Otherwise, all will suffer tribulation beyond everyone's recollection.
Excluded are those who escape the kill and continue in God's will.
God is my strong tower; I am the morning star and rule the nations with power.

Jezebel, with your hypnotic poison, will cause anyone to stumble.
I mute your voice and cast you down now so nothing else will crumble.
As the church of Thyatira, people take heed of this revelation.
There is no burden for the doctrine not in circulation.

Prayer

Lord, let Your will be done on earth as it is in heaven. May Your spirit be in the hearts of all preachers, teachers, prophets, apostles, evangelists, and those of the secular world. Please let us use Your gifts in the most excellent way where You get the glory. In Jesus's name, I pray. Amen.

PRACTICE: Replace the problem with God's promises by looking up the key phrase "A Godly Woman" in the Bible and applying the best scriptures that pertain to your situation. I have provided some scriptures below that you can use. Meditate on the promises until they reside in your spirit. Confess them out loud every time the problem tries to resurface.

Example: Problem – Jezebel / Promise – A Godly Woman

SCRIPTURES TO PONDER:

Titus 2:3-5 ~ 3 The older women likewise, that they be reverent in behavior, not slanderers, not given to much wine, teachers of good things 4 that they admonish the young women to love their husbands, to love their children, 5 to be discreet, chaste, homemakers, good, obedient to their own husbands, that the word of God may not be blasphemed (NKJV).

Proverbs 31:26 ~ She opens her mouth with wisdom; and on her tongue is the law of kindness (NKJV).

Proverbs 31:30 ~ Favor is deceitful, and beauty is vain: but a woman that feareth the Lord, she shall be praised.

1 Peter 3:15 ~ But sanctify the Lord God in your hearts: and be ready always to give an answer to every man that asketh you a reason of the hope that is in you with meekness and fear.

Ephesians 4:29 ~ Let no corrupt communication proceed out of your mouth, but that which is good to the use of edifying, that it may minister grace unto the hearers.

YOUR THOUGHTS:

_____
_____
_____
_____
_____
_____
_____
_____
_____
_____

HOW GREAT THE TEMPTATION

Blessed is the man that endureth temptation: for when he is tried,
he shall receive the crown of life,
Which the Lord hath promised to them that love him.
James 1:12

How can I get past what is common to man?
Welcoming my body to strangers was not part of the plan.
I know I am not to give it place,
Where it hungers to take up space.

My integrity you want to steal,
Even kill the personality I should reveal,
Bring destruction to that which was prearranged,
Which may lead me to be somewhat estranged.

Sensations answering my flesh's call,
No joy here when I am about to fall,
Making me feel as if I am on cloud nine,
This must be my secret valentine.

At first, I thought it was my friend,
An intimacy that's hard to comprehend.
Something I could not see was defiling me,
To a point where it was irritating, I decree.

Torment is what you bring to my soul.
A pull of life right out of me, is that your goal?

It felt right from the start, but the wrong remedy.
Wake up, this is a trick of the enemy.

This spouse of my spirit is a weight I need to lay aside.
The thought of it I can no longer hide.
He is wicked, sowing tares while I sleep.
Safe I want to be from a sickness I may reap.

My intention all along was to commit,
But God is faithful, I must admit.
This devil will flee from me as I resist,
I will escape or get Jesus to assist.

Prayer

Heavenly Father, give me the strength to avoid temptation when it comes my way. Please help me to bring my flesh under subjection so I can walk in Your spirit. In the name of Jesus I pray. Amen.

PRACTICE: Replace the problem with God's promises by looking up the keyword "temptation" in the Bible and applying the best scriptures that pertain to your situation. I have provided some scriptures below that you can use. Meditate on the promises until they reside in your spirit. Confess them out loud every time the problem tries to resurface.

Example: Problem – Temptation / Promise – Self-control

Dedra Johnson

SCRIPTURES TO PONDER:

1 Corinthians 10:13 ~ There hath no temptation taken you but such as is common to man: but God is faithful, who will not suffer you to be tempted above that ye are able; but will with the temptation also make a way to escape, that ye may be able to bear it.

James 4:7 ~ Submit yourselves therefore to God. Resist the devil, and he will flee from you.

Matthew 26:41 ~ Watch and pray, that ye enter not into temptation: the spirit indeed is willing, but the flesh is weak.

Ephesians 4:27 ~ Neither give place to the devil.

James 1:2 ~ My brethren, count it all joy when ye fall into divers temptations.

Hebrews 2:18 ~ For in that he himself hath suffered being tempted, he is able to succor them that are tempted.

YOUR THOUGHTS:

_____
_____
_____
_____
_____
_____
_____
_____
_____
_____
_____
_____

WHERE ARE YOU, MAN OF GOD?

For this cause shall a man leave his father and mother
and shall be joined unto his wife, and
they two shall be one flesh.
Ephesians 5:31

Will you obtain God's favor to have me, love me and not be bitter to me?
As Christ loved the church and gave Himself, will you do the same?
Where are you, man of God?

Am I your rib, almost joined at the hip, or from the same cup, sip?
Who will honor me as your wife to take on your name?
Where are you, man of God?

Can we dwell under the same roof, be heirs of the grace as divine proof?
Will we deal with this world with understanding or like it is a game?
Where are you, man of God?

Will you be my protector, provider, priest, prophet, and not a divider?
Can we accept our bodies as they are without being ashamed?
Where are you, man of God?

Can we agree and choose the better as we pray and dine together?
Can we just enjoy each other to the fullest, never putting out the flame?
Where are you, man of God?

Where I am the apple of your eye, in silence learning the Word until I die?
Where I am resilient and show how I overcame?
Where are you, man of God?

Do you have a love for God and yourself with a zeal; my children and I are a package deal?
Will you always have my back? This I will acclaim.
Where are you, man of God?

Can we be the examples others will mirror; together conquer challenges in every area?
A love that will forever soar is what we will proclaim.
Man of God, come and rescue me.

Prayer

Lord God, help us to have the spouse in which you have designed for us. Please help us to have a true family built on love and follow its structure as you have ordained. In the name of Jesus I pray. Amen.

PRACTICE: Replace the problem with God's promises by looking up the keyword "husband" in the Bible and applying the best scriptures that pertain to your situation. I have provided some scriptures below that you can use. Meditate on the promises until they reside in your spirit. Confess them out loud every time the problem tries to resurface.

Example: Problem – Fornication / Promise – Husband

SCRIPTURES TO PONDER:

Proverbs 18:22 ~ Whoso findeth a wife findeth a good thing, and obtaineth favor of the Lord.

Ephesians 5:25 ~ Husbands, love your wives, even as Christ also loved the church, and gave himself for it.

1 Corinthians 7:2-3 ~ 2 Nevertheless, to avoid fornication, let every man have his own wife, and let every woman have her own husband. Let the husband render unto the wife due benevolence: and likewise also the wife unto the husband.

2 Corinthians 6:14 ~ Be ye not unequally yoked together with unbelievers: for what fellowship hath righteousness with unrighteousness? And what communion hath light with darkness?

1 Peter 3:1 ~ Likewise, ye wives, be in subjection to your own husbands; that, if any obey not the word, they also may without the word be won by the conversation of the wives;

1 Peter 3:7 ~ Likewise, ye husbands, dwell with them according to knowledge, giving honor unto the wife, as unto the weaker vessel, and as being heirs together of the grace of life; that your prayers be not hindered.

YOUR THOUGHTS:

_____
_____
_____
_____
_____
_____
_____
_____
_____
_____
_____
_____
_____

GROWING IN PERFECTION

__Therefore you are to be perfect, as your heavenly Father is perfect.__
__Matthew 5:48__

No more will I be carried away by man's words and ways.
Restoration is all I crave no matter what you may say.
I have strength in the areas that were once my shortcomings.
Mind, body, and soul, now I am forever becoming.

My struggles fortified the foundation laid.
To God be the glory for the price His Son, Jesus, paid.
I was spiritually dead, then brought back to life,
Just a little skeptical in being another man's wife.

Wholeness is what I sought, so vital was mind renewal.
Doing God's will shaped me into the perfect jewel.
No shame in what I hoped for as I purified myself,
Studying the Bible instead of leaving it on the shelf.

I have tasted and seen how good God can be,
Turn back, oh no! I shall stay on bended knees.
God is perfect, just, pure, righteous, and faithful,
What I strive to be since I am exceedingly grateful.

It is me, being trained to perfection, the Holy Spirit will thrust
To be a partaker of grace and remind me in God to trust.
I have His love in my heart;
I am not embarrassed of being set apart.

All the things that defile our flesh and spirit have got to go.
This is how true holiness is perfected without putting on a show.
Evil is wrong and something God hates, so we must reject.
Compromise is out of the question and should not be a subject.

My fruit is evidence to others that I am blessed.
I know how to restore a soul in gentleness.
I am quick to detect an error and be more effective spiritually.
My focus is set in getting ready for eternity.

Prayer

Oh Lord, help us to grow in Your perfection knowing that we must endure suffering to develop Your character as we find hope in You. Please bring transformation unto us where we eat the meat of Your Word and not drink its milk. In the name of Jesus I pray. Amen.

PRACTICE: Replace the problem with God's promises by looking up the keyword "perfection" in the Bible and applying the best scriptures that pertain to your situation. I have provided some scriptures below that you can use. Meditate on the promises until they reside in your spirit. Confess them out loud every time the problem tries to resurface.

Example: Problem – Imperfection / Promise – Perfection

SCRIPTURES TO PONDER:

James 1:4 ~ But let patience have her perfect work, that ye may be perfect and entire, wanting nothing.

Psalms 118:8 ~ It is better to trust in the Lord than to put confidence in man.

Dedra Johnson

2 Corinthians 7:1 ~ Having therefore these promises, dearly beloved, let us cleanse ourselves from all filthiness of the flesh and spirit, perfecting holiness in the fear of God.

1 Timothy 4:12 ~ Let no man despise thy youth; but be thou an example of the believers, in word, in conversation, in charity, in spirit, in faith, in purity.

Psalms 34:8 ~ O taste and see that the Lord is good: blessed is the man that trusteth in him.

1 Peter 1:16 ~ Because it is written, be ye holy; for I am holy.

YOUR THOUGHTS:

_____
_____
_____
_____
_____
_____
_____
_____
_____
_____
_____
_____
_____
_____
_____
_____
_____
_____
_____

TAKE YOUR HANDS OFF MY INHERITANCE

***Blessed are they which are persecuted for righteousness' sake:
for theirs is the kingdom of heaven.***
Matthew 5:10

I will not let you deceive me.
It is the truth that has set me free.
My soul, I will not forsake.
Careful I will be of the advice I intake.

The world I must unfriend and cut all ties.
I can't be God's enemy where He will not abide.
My faith alone reminds me of my benefits.
I do not care if I am in your book a misfit.

It was grace that saved me, my true ace.
I have laid aside many weights in this race.
I am in wait of the hope of righteousness.
I will not settle for any of your unrighteousness.

Authorizing lust, hate, or intoxication to cause me to stumble,
Waste not your energy, I must stay humble.
You are not going to make me be angry or sexually immoral,
Nor worship idols and touch filth, that rebuke will be oral.

Against God rebel, steal, and operate in jealousy.
Be a part of your deception, you must be crazy!

I look forward to inheriting God's kingdom.
I am aware it may lead to martyrdom.

Wisdom will always win over shame.
What you do won't hurt my name.
All you rushed to possess will perish.
My legacy for my descendants will be left to cherish.

Endurance I have gained through my trouble.
Because I am just, I expect double.
In that land of promise, I will forever dwell,
Surely to hear God say, "You have done well."

Prayer

Lord, thank You for Your grace. I am grateful in knowing that Satan has loosed everything that You have for me. Please give me the strength to hold on until You come. In your son Jesus's name I pray. Amen.

PRACTICE: Replace the problem with God's promises by looking up the keyword "inheritance" in the Bible and applying the best scriptures that pertain to your situation. I have provided some scriptures below that you can use. Meditate on the promises until they reside in your spirit. Confess them out loud every time the problem tries to resurface.

Example: Problem – Covetousness / Promise – Inheritance

SCRIPTURES TO PONDER:

Proverbs 13:22 ~ A good man leaveth an inheritance to his children's children: and the wealth of the sinner is laid up for the just.

Psalms 37:29 ~ The righteous shall inherit the land, and dwell therein forever.

Proverbs 17:2 ~ A wise servant shall have rule over a son that causeth shame, and shall have part of the inheritance among the brethren.

John 3:5 ~ Jesus answered, Verily, verily, I say unto thee, Except a man be born of water and of the Spirit, he cannot enter into the kingdom of God.

Galatians 5:19-21 ~ Now the works of the flesh are manifest, which are these; adultery, fornication, uncleanness, lasciviousness, idolatry, witchcraft, hatred, variance, emulations, wrath, strife, seditions, heresies, envyings, murders, drunkenness, revellings, and such like: of the which I tell you before, as I have also told you in time past, that they which do such things shall not inherit the kingdom of God.

YOUR THOUGHTS:

_____
_____
_____
_____
_____
_____
_____
_____
_____
_____
_____
_____

WISDOM TO FACE MY DEMONS

Happy is the man that findeth wisdom, and the man that getteth understanding.
Proverbs 3:13

So anxious I was to do my own thing,
Contrary to Your divine will in my being.
All I had to do was pray, apply Your Word,
And give thanks as I am cut by the sword.

With the fear that my beliefs would not manifest,
My surroundings were totally opposite of the best.
I could do this. I have power, love, and a mind that is sound,
To get up and bounce back even when I fall down.

The path you blocked to keep me from being punctual on my job,
To complete my assignments or my virtues you tried to rob.
Other things in my life you sabotaged, yet I am still nice.
Don't you know I can do all things through Christ?

Putting my faith to work although my body is under attack,
Growths here and there I wish to disappear and never come back.
The pain you release to remind me of what has been already revealed,
More convinced in my spirit that by Jesus's stripes I am healed.

Lack must go when I am believing God for provision.
Lust wants to keep me bound and confused to receive instruction.
Bid high or bid low, I cannot be bought.
By choice, not chance, I enter into that rest no one sought.

Outraged I was in my anger, I am now careful of what I say.
Bitter then sweet, I had to forgive before the end of the day.
Many potholes I have hit, but holiness was the route to my calling.
Diligent I am about my Father's business, I have to stop stalling.

Why perish for something I do not know,
In a world of technology that is never slow?
Using godly wisdom is forever changing my story,
As well as making my inheritance glory.

Prayer

Father God, help us to seek You first in all that we do or turn to the Holy Bible. There is no problem You cannot solve. Please let us not despise wisdom and instruction. In the name of Jesus I pray. Amen.

PRACTICE: Replace the problem with God's promises by looking up the keyword "wisdom" in the Bible and applying the best scriptures that pertain to your situation. I have provided some scriptures below that you can use. Meditate on the promises until they reside in your spirit. Confess them out loud every time the problem tries to resurface.
Example: Problem – Foolishness / Promise – Wisdom

SCRIPTURES TO PONDER:

Proverbs 19:20 ~ Hear counsel, and receive instruction, that thou mayest be wise in thy latter end.

Philippians 4:13 ~ I can do all things through Christ which strengthens me (NKJV).

Philippians 4:19 ~ But my God shall supply all your need according to His riches in glory by Christ Jesus.

2 Timothy 1:7 ~ For God hath not given us the spirit of fear; but of power, and of love, and of a sound mind.

Isaiah 53:5 ~ But He was wounded for our transgressions, He was bruised for our iniquities: the chastisement of our peace was upon Him; and with His stripes we are healed.

James 1:5 ~ If any of you lack wisdom, let him ask of God, that giveth to all men liberally, and upbraideth not; and it shall be given him.

YOUR THOUGHTS:

_____
_____
_____
_____
_____
_____
_____
_____
_____
_____
_____
_____
_____
_____
_____
_____
_____
_____

GRACED

*But the God of all grace, who hath called us unto his
eternal glory by Christ Jesus,
after that ye have suffered a while, make you perfect,
stablish, strengthen, and settle you.*
1 Peter 5:10

I am saved by grace; it is no mistake.
I thought my heritage would be at stake.
Sin, you are no longer my master.
My attitude is different as I encounter a disaster.

A wearied life armed for battle yet births a new song,
In a world where wrong is right and right is wrong.
Lord, thank you for chastising me when I get out of line,
The perfect example of love extended from a true vine.

Your supernatural strength takes effect in my weakness.
One's spirit, soul, and body aligned with the Holy Spirit's fullness,
Ignites God's kingdom here on earth like an eagle taking wings.
Without You, Jesus, I can do nothing, You are my King.

Pride, go away; low I must be to receive God's favor.
Reliance on Him protects me from doing vain labor.
I am graced to do so much that is effortless.
Credit I cannot take then turn around and be merciless.

Salvation is for everyone, but you must accept it,
Be the salt while here and be a light in a pit.

Where there is evil, grace will help you do what is ethical.
The way God works is so amazing and mystical.

I have endured what others have died from or had them bound.
I have dealt with some that others cannot stand to be around,
Or be in areas where others do not want to be.
Come now, that life of abundance flowing with milk and honey.

Prayer

Dear God, may we obtain access by faith into this grace in which we stand, and may we rejoice in hope of the glory of God. In Jesus's name I pray. Amen.

PRACTICE: Replace the problem with God's promises by looking up the keyword "grace" in the Bible and applying the best scriptures that pertain to your situation. I have provided some scriptures below that you can use. Meditate on the promises until they reside in your spirit. Confess them out loud every time the problem tries to resurface.

Example: Problem – Disfavor / Promise – Grace

SCRIPTURES TO PONDER:

Ephesians 2:8 ~ For by grace are ye saved through faith; and that not of yourselves: it is the gift of God.

Romans 6:14 ~ For sin shall not have dominion over you: for ye are not under the law, but under grace.

John 15:5 ~ I am the vine, ye are the branches: He that abideth in me, and I in him, the same bringeth forth much fruit: for without me ye can do nothing.

Numbers 14:8 ~ If the Lord delight in us, then he will bring us into this land, and give it us; a land which floweth with milk and honey.

James 4:6 ~ But he giveth more grace. Wherefore he saith, God resisteth the proud, but giveth grace unto the humble.

Titus 2:11 ~ For the grace of God that bringeth salvation hath appeared to all men.

YOUR THOUGHTS:

WHO AM I?

But he that is joined unto the LORD is one spirit.
1 Corinthians 6:17

I am a child of the GREAT I AM, for I am who God says I am.
I am that light in the earth that shines bright, just as I walk by faith and not by sight.
I am the one who will walk in her due season without your approval for no given reason.
I am an ambassador of Christ; I am more than a conqueror through the one who paid the price.
I am the healed, the delivered, the overcomer; I am for sure that late bloomer.

I am a believer full of dreams; I can do all things because I am redeemed.
I am sanctified by the Holy Ghost, I am righteous and persecuted by most.
I am the one who has set her face; I am a hearer and doer of God's Word, ready for the race.
I am the head and not the tail, I am above and not beneath refusing to fail.
I am a lender and a borrower I will not be; I am a receiver of what God has for me.

I am saved by grace through faith, definitely not moved by those who hate.
I am that tree planted by rivers of waters, though sent out like a sheep to be slaughtered.

I am the one whose heart was pierced by an arrow, but I am of more value than many sparrows.
I am that virtuous "P31" woman; I am beloved with fear of no man.
I am a seeker of the kingdom; I am a possessor of peace and godly wisdom.

I am blessed and highly favored; I am full of joy in my labor.
I am a survivor of the scriptures that give life; I am an anointed vessel without strife.
I am protected with God's armor; I am a fervent prayer warrior.
I am holy and profuse; I am set apart for the Master's use.
I may have been delayed, but not denied when betrayed.

Prayer

Heavenly Father, You know me better than I know myself. Help me to know who I am in You. Let me not look to others for my identity. In Jesus's name I pray. Amen.

PRACTICE: Replace the problem with God's promises by looking up the keyword "identity" in the Bible and applying the best scriptures that pertain to your situation. I have provided some scriptures below that you can use. Meditate on the promises until they reside in your spirit. Confess them out loud every time the problem tries to resurface.
Example: Problem – Misidentify / Promise – Identity

SCRIPTURES TO PONDER:

Ephesians 2:10 ~ For we are his workmanship, created in Christ Jesus unto good works, which God hath before ordained that we should walk in them.

1 John 4:4 ~ Ye are of God, little children, and have overcome them: because greater is he that is in you, than he that is in the world.

Psalms 1:3 ~ And he shall be like a tree planted by the rivers of water, that bringeth forth his fruit in his season; his leaf also shall not wither; and whatsoever he doeth shall prosper.

Ephesians 4:22-24 That ye put off concerning the former conversation the old man, which is corrupt according to the deceitful lusts; And be renewed in the spirit of your mind; And that ye put on the new man, which after God is created in righteousness and true holiness.

2 Corinthians 5:17 ~ Therefore if any man be in Christ, he is a new creature: old things are passed away; behold, all things are become new.

James 1:22 ~ But be ye doers of the word, and not hearers only, deceiving your own selves.

YOUR THOUGHTS:

_____
_____
_____
_____
_____
_____
_____
_____
_____
_____
_____
_____
_____
_____
_____
_____

THE CHALLENGE OF MATURING IN GOD

You are all sons of God through faith in Christ Jesus.
Galatians 3:26

Young or old, maturity is required of me.
I believe in Jesus and receive Him; misperception of this process should not be.
His power I try to utilize but lack the results I expected.
Overwhelmed by frustration and anxiety, it did not matter whom I affected.

My eyes are fixed on God's promises, but how long is this wait?
Though sidetracked by temptation, I will not remain anybody's bait.
I know I am blessed, yet I live from paycheck to paycheck.
A peacemaker I am, but anger stirs my soul to a total wreck.

I want to be Spirit-led, but deficiency is present in my discernment.
Not dealing with my own demons led to my imprisonment.
We are to test the spirit by the spirit and see if it is of God.
I dare bear a glory where one might say "Ichabod".

It has not been revealed what I will be, so why do I fear what is in my future?
Developing in the image of Christ is definitely the result of my adventure.
Criticism, lies, and mistreatment have made me slip in my love walk.
Diligently, I try to do what is right and not just talk the talk.

Dedra Johnson

The struggle of depending on others to pray for me when I can do it myself,
To sit under a pastor, learn from him, and become a pastor myself,
To say God loves me then have second thoughts because of my experiences,
I am stretched above and beyond to be that godly influence.

Hardship I did endure, yet I am thankful, and I sing with praise,
Not considering the witnesses or how they gaze.
I cannot change people, so to avoid the drama, I hide.
With confidence, I rest because God is on my side.

Carefully, I distinguish good from evil eliminating any disqualifications.
I work the Word by faith to help validate my sanctification.
Discouraged I am when one rejects what I have planted in his or her life.
I am sure that someone will water the seed and bring hope instead of strife.

Prayer

Lord, help us to grow more in You. Please give us the courage to face any life challenge. Thank You for being our strength. In Jesus's name I pray. Amen.

PRACTICE: Replace the problem with God's promises by looking up the keyword "maturity" in the Bible and applying the best scriptures that pertain to your situation. I have provided some scriptures below that you can use. Meditate on the promises until they reside in your spirit. Confess them out loud every time the problem tries to resurface.

Example: Problem – Immaturity / Promise – Maturity

SCRIPTURES TO PONDER:

1 Corinthians 13:11 ~ When I was a child, I spake as a child, I understood as a child, I thought as a child: but when I became a man, I put away childish things.

Ephesians 6:10 ~ Finally, my brethren, be strong in the Lord, and in the power of his might.

1 John 4:1 ~ Beloved, believe not every spirit, but try the spirits whether they are of God: because many false prophets are gone out into the world.

Proverbs 3:5 ~ Trust in the Lord with all thine heart; and lean not unto thine own understanding.

Romans 12:21 ~ Be not overcome of evil, but overcome evil with good.

2 Timothy 2:3 ~ Thou therefore endure hardness, as a good soldier of Jesus Christ.

YOUR THOUGHTS:

DO YOU HAVE THE CHARACTER?

Be ye therefore perfect, even as your Father which is in heaven is perfect.
Matthew 5:48

To be ungrateful for every blessing when you should be thankful,
To have failure pull you by a rope when you should have hope,
To judge my outer parts rather than the inner man of my heart,
Is that what you call character?

To disrespect me, entice my spouse, then try to take my house,
To be full of so much evil towards me that you turn my kids against me,
To manipulate through actions, what you say, and attempt to get your way,
Is that what you call character?

To keep me busy doing your work and still want to stab me with a fork,
To expect a promotion when you are not qualified for the position,
To be accountable for your mistakes, and not go jump into a lake,
Is that what you call character?

To offer you my help in kindness, then you abuse me out of blindness,
To be critical of everything as you live and not be quick to forgive,
To walk out of integrity when no one is looking or in adversity,
Is that what you call character?

To bear what you should fix, you know good and evil do not mix,
To influence me to be a pervert when I am sold-out to Christ to convert,

No Longer Bound

To drink with you, Satan, I will not do or eat and jeopardize my judgment seat,
Is that what you call character?

To uphold a good name as I walk in love and peace without shame,
To be created so unique that you are different even in your physique,
To receive man's favor and release the fragrance of your Savior,
Is that what you call character?

To love when wronged even if the time is prolonged,
To keep quiet in conflict no matter how severe you want to afflict,
To be honest when you want to lie then break every ungodly soul tie,
Now that is what you call character!

Prayer

Oh Heavenly Father, would You please give me the character to do what is necessary to keep every blessing You give me? Help me to start right so I can end right. In Jesus's name I pray. Amen.

PRACTICE: Replace the problem with God's promises by looking up the keyword "character" in the Bible and applying the best scriptures that pertain to your situation. I have provided some scriptures below that you can use. Meditate on the promises until they reside in your spirit. Confess them out loud every time the problem tries to resurface.

Example: Problem – Immorality / Promise – Character

SCRIPTURES TO PONDER:

2 Timothy 3:16 ~ All scripture is given by inspiration of God, and is profitable for doctrine, for reproof, for correction, for instruction in righteousness.

2 Peter 1:3 ~ According as his divine power hath given unto us all things that pertain unto life and godliness, through the knowledge of him that hath called us to glory and virtue.

Proverbs 22:1 ~ A good name is rather to be chosen than great riches, and loving favor rather than silver and gold.

Proverbs 10:9 ~ He that walketh uprightly walketh surely: but he that perverteth his ways shall be known.

1 Thessalonians 5:14 ~ Now we exhort you, brethren, warn them that are unruly, comfort the feebleminded, support the weak, be patient toward all men.

Colossians 3:17 ~ And whatsoever ye do in word or deed, do all in the name of the Lord Jesus, giving thanks to God and the Father by him.

YOUR THOUGHTS:

_____
_____
_____
_____
_____
_____
_____
_____
_____
_____
_____
_____
_____
_____

CHRIST, YOUR BRIDE AWAITS

*That he might present it to himself a glorious church,
not having spot, or wrinkle,
Or any such thing; but that it should be holy and
without blemish.*
Ephesians 5:27

You have given Yourself for us.
With no remorse, You covered our sin out of disgust.
On the other hand, I have given myself to earthly men,
Definitely aware that I was born again.

Ashamed I am that I am not your chaste virgin,
Though cleansed by Your spoken Word as my divine surgeon.
I am all Yours; I am holy, redeemed, and perfect.
This link I will let no man disconnect.

I wait for You to rejoice over me.
I appreciate that You would not just let me be.
Oh, how You have loved me and kept me from harm,
Especially when I am faced with a storm.

I am thirsty for You; I take the water of life without a price.
Gamble my life, no way, I dare one roll any dice.
In obedience, I imitate You as I follow your footsteps,
Learning from my sufferings while building a rep.

Unto You, I submit every part of my being.
I am Your queen; You are my King.

In reverence, I must bow at Your feet,
Welcoming You with an informal greet.

On your return, let all the trumpets sound aloud.
Glad we will be the moment You appear in the clouds.
My flesh is crucified so my body will be glorious and new.
Come, my husband, for I have made myself ready for You.

Prayer

Lord God, thank You for giving Your son, Jesus as a ransom for us. Help us to die to our flesh so we will grow into His image in this earthly process. In Jesus's name I pray. Amen.

PRACTICE: Replace the problem with God's promises by looking up the key phrase "the bride of Christ" in the Bible and applying the best scriptures that pertain to your situation. I have provided some scriptures below that you can use. Meditate on the promises until they reside in your spirit. Confess them out loud every time the problem tries to resurface.

> Example: Problem – the bride of Satan /
> Promise – the bride of Christ

SCRIPTURES TO PONDER:

2 Corinthians 11:2 ~ For I am jealous over you with godly jealousy: for I have espoused you to one husband, that I may present you as a chaste virgin to Christ.

Ezekiel 16:8 ~ Now when I passed by thee, and looked upon thee, behold, thy time was the time of love; and I spread my skirt over thee, and covered thy nakedness: yea, I sware unto thee, and entered into a covenant with thee, saith the Lord GOD, and thou becamest mine.

1 Corinthians 1:10 ~ Now I beseech you, brethren, by the name of our Lord Jesus Christ, that ye all speak the same thing, and that there be no divisions among you; but that ye be perfectly joined together in the same mind and in the same judgment.

Revelation 19:7 ~ Let us be glad and rejoice, and give honor to him: for the marriage of the Lamb is come, and his wife hath made herself ready.

Revelation 22:17 ~ And the Spirit and the bride say, Come. And let him that heareth say, Come. And let him that is athirst come. And whosoever will, let him take the water of life freely.

Hebrews 12:28 ~ Wherefore we receiving a kingdom which cannot be moved, let us have grace, whereby we may serve God acceptably with reverence and godly fear.

YOUR THOUGHTS:

_____
_____
_____
_____
_____
_____
_____
_____
_____
_____
_____
_____
_____
_____

WHEN THE INNER MAN CRIES OUT

Create in me a clean heart, O God;
and renew a right spirit within me.
Psalms 51:10

Lord, I look to You to make up for the missing pieces in me;
That which caused my downfall is what surrounds me, should this be?
The same spirit we all share being comfortable with that which is familiar,
But I want out of this aggravation since we were called to be peculiar.

Body going through the motions of an enduring pain that is residual,
I have to get rid of the root cause of this unseen individual.
A wolf I sense you are, pretending to be a sheep,
No warning, no alarm, no sound of a beep.

Upon my wretched soul, you have crept,
My silent cry is "Help, help, help!"
My love, you have taken for granted,
My drive to kill you with kindness was all I wanted.

A true warrior ready for battle I am regardless of the exhaustion.
For enough is enough, I am down, and you ask no questions.
You kick me like an empty can found on the ground.
Do not get mad if I retaliate to keep from being bound.

I know I am in my flesh when I should be walking in the Spirit,
But misery does not need any company when someone may get hit.
Guide me, oh Lord, to be that lamp in which everyone looks upon.
I am aware of what I need, so from Your presence I can no longer run.

Nowhere can I trace You, but I know You are there.
A teacher does not talk during the test, but I know You care.
That which is unclean in my heart defiles all.
I have got to have You, God, to avoid this fall.

Your love is so powerful I give You the upper hand.
With Your embrace, I could cross burning sand.
Nothing I can think of can compare.
God, You have won the life You spared.

Prayer

Heavenly Father, I thank You for knowing the intentions of my heart. Help me to reach my destiny by overcoming every obstacle. In the name of Jesus I pray. Amen.

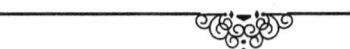

PRACTICE: Replace the problem with God's promises by looking up the key phrase "inner man" in the Bible and applying the best scriptures that pertain to your situation. I have provided some scriptures below that you can use. Meditate on the promises until they reside in your spirit. Confess them out loud every time the problem tries to resurface.

Example: Problem – Outer man / Promise – Inner man

SCRIPTURES TO PONDER:

Ephesians 3:16 ~ That he would grant you, according to the riches of his glory, to be strengthened with might by his Spirit in the inner man.

Proverbs 20:27 ~ The spirit of man is the lamp of the Lord, searching all the innermost parts of his being.

2 Corinthians 3:18 ~ But we all, with unveiled face, beholding as in a mirror the glory of the Lord, are being transformed into the same image from glory to glory, just as from the Lord, the Spirit.

Matthew 7:15 ~ Beware of false prophets, which come to you in sheep's clothing, but inwardly they are ravening wolves.

2 Peter 1:4 ~ Whereby are given unto us exceeding great and precious promises: that by these ye might be partakers of the divine nature, having escaped the corruption that is in the world through lust.

2 Corinthians 1:20 ~ For all the promises of God in him are yea, and in him Amen, unto the glory of God by us.

YOUR THOUGHTS:

_____
_____
_____
_____
_____
_____
_____
_____
_____
_____

THE WEIGHT OF FORGIVING WRONG

And be ye kind one to another, tenderhearted,
forgiving one another,
even as God for Christ's sake hath forgiven you.
Ephesians 4:32

I am going through, but to whom do I turn to?
On several occasions, I tried to confide in you.
Your mouth was used to bring humiliation,
To be used by Satan to tear down my character and reputation.

Disappointment and failure have joined hands to toast.
Encouraging words were what I needed most;
No sympathy is wanted, just an ear to hear what I have to say.
No matter what you do, I choose to forgive each day.

To continue to be friends or cut you loose is my choice.
Being nonchalant is my stance; don't be so quick to rejoice.
Staying is not an option when lack of value is my excuse.
True love covers sin and brings change, not persistent abuse.

I thought agreement from both parties was the deal.
I will put all my trust in the Lord who is real.
The woman caught in adultery was not condemned.
Her obedience to the command of Jesus resolved that problem.

My motive is to do the will of God instead of my own.
To be compassionate, bless, pray, and help, not beat to the bone.

Your motives you carefully hid knowing they were forbidden.
Strings you tried to attach, but your decision was overridden.

In God's hands, I leave you for your stubbornness and defiance.
Everything we had crumbled because of no reliance.
How blind I was to the truth even from my youth,
Now left to correct every wrong before the Almighty One, feeling aloof.

Prayer

Lord, thank You for forgiving me. I have been wronged by others and I need Your help to make it through. I cannot do this alone. Please help me to forgive. In Jesus's name I pray. Amen.

PRACTICE: Replace the problem with God's promises by looking up the keyword "forgiveness" in the Bible and applying the best scriptures that pertain to your situation. I have provided some scriptures below that you can use. Meditate on the promises until they reside in your spirit. Confess them out loud every time the problem tries to resurface.

Example: Problem – Unforgiveness / Promise – Forgiveness

SCRIPTURES TO PONDER:

1 John 1:9 ~ If we confess our sins, he is faithful and just to forgive us our sins, and to cleanse us from all unrighteousness.

James 5:16 ~ Confess your faults one to another, and pray one for another, that ye may be healed. The effectual fervent prayer of a righteous man availeth much.

Luke 6:27-28 ~ 27 But I say unto you which hear, Love your enemies, do good to them which hate you, 28 Bless them that curse you, and pray for them which despitefully use you.

Proverbs 10:12 ~ Hatred stirs up strife: but love covers all sins (NKJV).

John 8:10-11 ~ 10 When Jesus had lifted up himself, and saw none but the woman, he said unto her, Woman, where are those thine accusers? Hath no man condemned thee? 11 She said, No man, Lord. And Jesus said unto her, neither do I condemn thee: go, and sin no more.

Jeremiah 29:11 ~ For I know the thoughts that I think toward you, saith the Lord, thoughts of peace, and not of evil, to give you an expected end.

YOUR THOUGHTS:

THE OUTLOOK OF RESTORATION

And I will restore to you the years that the locust hath eaten, the cankerworm, and the caterpillar, and the palmerworm, my great army which I sent among you.
Joel 2:25

Long-suffering, I have tasted of your bitter cup,
To God, though He seems distant, I look up.
Restoration in my health and soul I would adore.
I have made believing as strenuous as a chore.

My faith has caused me to be victorious,
Regardless of the declarations Satan tried to make notorious.
Thank you, Lord, that I am refined, purged, and purified,
Being so full of Your Spirit that I almost cried.

Not tears of sadness because of the process, but of joy,
God considered a broken vessel like me and even you to employ.
Patiently, I wait to receive double for my shame,
Reversing the pain to hope in the change of my name.

It took acknowledging my wrongs to turn in the way I would not regret.
I desired, I prayed, and I believed to receive everything I should beget.
Nothing can move me from having the confidence of what God can do.
If He allowed me to go through anything, He will bring me out of it too.

Hope, love, and peace are in my future.
I refuse to bow to the minor when I can have the major that will nurture.
My heart I now protect for it is of flesh and no longer of stone.
I am careful of whom I let get close to me since I am in a new zone.

Drama, you have no control over me since you are a troublemaker.
You influence for the worst . . . a great taker and a genuine faker.
If you lack support, inspiration, and motivation,
Consider yourself outside of my inner circle; I refuse to have any stagnation.

Free of guilt, my soul can rest from damnation,
Anxious I am to see God pour out His Spirit on every nation.
Faithful is He in cleansing us of all wickedness,
Though transformation begins with correction in meekness.

Prayer

Lord, I thank You for being a God of restoration. Would You please help me to regain everything that was lost in my fiery trials? In Jesus's name I pray. Amen.

PRACTICE: Replace the problem with God's promises by looking up the keyword "restoration" in the Bible and applying the best scriptures that pertain to your situation. I have provided some scriptures below that you can use. Meditate on the promises until they reside in your spirit. Confess them out loud every time the problem tries to resurface.

Example: Problem – Destruction / Promise – Restoration

Dedra Johnson

SCRIPTURES TO PONDER:

John 15:7 ~ If ye abide in me, and my words abide in you, ye shall ask what ye will, and it shall be done unto you.

Jeremiah 30:17 ~ For I will restore health unto thee, and I will heal thee of thy wounds, saith the LORD. Because they called thee an Outcast, saying, this is Zion, whom no man seeketh after.

Isaiah 61:7 ~ For your shame ye shall have double; and for confusion they shall rejoice in their portion: therefore in their land they shall possess the double: everlasting joy shall be unto them.

3 John 1:2 ~ Beloved, I wish above all things that thou mayest prosper and be in health, even as thy soul prospereth.

1 John 1:7 ~ But if we walk in the light, as he is in the light, we have fellowship one with another, and the blood of Jesus Christ his Son cleanseth us from all sin.

1 John 5:4 ~ For whatsoever is born of God overcometh the world: and this is the victory that overcometh the world, even our faith.

YOUR THOUGHTS:

_____
_____
_____
_____
_____
_____
_____
_____

I AM RUTH

And Ruth said, "Entreat me not to leave you, or
to turn back from following after you;
for wherever you go, I will go; and
wherever you lodge, I will lodge;
your people shall be my people,
and your God, my God."
Ruth 1:16 (NKJV)

One of the greatest love stories in the bible was written about me, a native of the Moabites.
Out of curiosity of trying something new, I left my family and married an Israelite.
I lost my father-in-law, my brother-in-law, and my husband, such a tragedy.
Who am I? I am Ruth, Ruth you see.

I was saddened and almost thought all hope was gone.
I could not leave my mother-in-law, Naomi, alone.
I became her shadow, her follower, and server of her divinity.
Who am I? I am Ruth, Ruth you see.

Oh, how bitter Naomi became for the death of her spouse and two sons.
Back to her hometown of Bethlehem, she was drawn.
I helped out by gleaning in a nearby barley field for food to escape poverty.
Who am I? I am Ruth, Ruth you see.

The field belonged to a relative of Naomi's deceased husband.
His name was Boaz and the one God used to show His hand.
Somehow, of all the gleaners, he noticed and favored me.
Who am I? I am Ruth, Ruth you see.

Immediately, Naomi advised me on what I should do for provision.
I fell at the feet of Boaz, my kinsman-redeemer in submission.
No more worries in this life I had because he took me as his wife-to-be.
Who am I? I am Ruth, Ruth you see.

From this union came our son, Obed, the grandfather of King David.
I was the great-grandmother of a warrior king no man outdid.
I was the ancestor of Jesus who came to save you and me.
Who am I? I am Ruth, Ruth you see.

Prayer

Heavenly Father, You are wonderful in all of Your ways. Please give us the kind of favor You gave Ruth with Boaz. Let us know what it truly feels like to be loved unconditionally. In the name of Jesus I pray. Amen.

PRACTICE: Replace the problem with God's promises by looking up the keyword "favor" in the Bible and applying the best scriptures that pertain to your situation. I have provided some scriptures below that you can use. Meditate on the promises until they reside in your spirit. Confess them out loud every time the problem tries to resurface.
Example: Problem – Disfavor / Promise – Favor

SCRIPTURES TO PONDER:

Psalms 5:12 ~ For thou, Lord, wilt bless the righteous; with favor wilt thou compass him as with a shield.

Psalms 90:17 ~ And let the beauty of the Lord our God be upon us: and establish thou the work of our hands upon us; yea, the work of our hands establish thou it.

Psalms 30:5 ~ For his anger endureth but a moment; in his favor is life: weeping may endure for a night, but joy cometh in the morning.

Ruth 2:8 ~ Then said Boaz unto Ruth, "Hearest thou not, my daughter? Go not to glean in another field, neither go from hence, but abide here fast by my maidens."

Ruth 4:10 ~ Moreover Ruth the Moabitess, the wife of Mahlon, have I purchased to be my wife, to raise up the name of the dead upon his inheritance, that the name of the dead be not cut off from among his brethren, and from the gate of his place: ye are witnesses this day.

Proverbs 3:33 ~ The curse of the LORD is in the house of the wicked: but he blesseth the habitation of the just.

YOUR THOUGHTS:

HOW LONG WILL YOU REJECT ME?

He came unto his own, and his own received him not.
John 1:11

Do you not know who I am? I am Alpha and Omega, the beginning and the end.
You thought you could bypass Me to get to my Daddy, now that I did not recommend.
He loves you so much that He sent Me not to condemn you but to save you and live abundantly.
How long will you reject Me?

Do you not believe that I am the redeemer? All I ask is that you love, for it never fails.
Put away the ministry of death written in stone; I have fulfilled the law so grace will prevail.
On the cross, I died at Calvary for your sin, dominion, healing, prosperity, and peace.
How long will you reject Me?

Am I not the author and the finisher of your faith? I have torn the veil so I can be your intercessor.
My Father will hear your case to do the impossible. Did you forget that I was the miracle worker?
I have also given you the power to do what I have done and greater so Satan will flee.
How long will you reject Me?

Are you willing to take the limits off? Let me bless you beyond your dreams.
Stop living your life as you planned it and do what has been asked of you from the Supreme.
I am here to pick you up if you fall; you are in good hands with the Holy Trinity.
How long will you reject Me?

Will you believe and receive what I have already done for you to have success?
Many may cause you to do something you should not do in this process.
I do not want you to feel like you have to hide your face, I am full of mercy.
How long will you reject Me?

Realize God is with you; He will never leave you or forsake you.
Walk in love, which can only be done with help from above.
Receive salvation, for you know not the day or the hour of death's visitation.
So stop rejecting me!

Embrace God's grace. This is vital in successfully running the Christian race.
Accept My Rest. For only My Father knows what is best.
Receive My Favor. This is My promise to you when you decide to make Me your Lord and savior.
So stop rejecting me, stop rejecting me; for the last time, I said stop rejecting me!

Prayer

Heavenly Father, help us to accept Your Son, Jesus. We cannot live in this world without a savior. In the name of Jesus I pray. Amen.

PRACTICE: Replace the problem with God's promises by looking up the keyword "rejection" or "acceptance" in the Bible and applying the best scriptures that pertain to your situation. I have provided some scriptures below that you can use. Meditate on the promises until they reside in your spirit. Confess them out loud every time the problem tries to resurface.

Example: Problem – Rejection / Promise – Acceptance

SCRIPTURES TO PONDER:

Luke 6:22 ~ Blessed are ye, when men shall hate you, and when they shall separate you from their company, and shall reproach you, and cast out your name as evil, for the Son of man's sake.

Romans 15:7 ~ Wherefore receive ye one another, as Christ also received us to the glory of God.

Romans 8:28 ~ And we know that all things work together for good to them that love God, to them who are the called according to his purpose.

Romans 8:31 ~ What shall we then say to these things? If God be for us, who can be against us?

Matthew 10:14 ~ And whosoever shall not receive you, nor hear your words, when ye depart out of that house or city, shake off the dust of your feet.

YOUR THOUGHTS:

_____
_____
_____
_____
_____

APPENDIX 1

The Practice Guide

The purpose of this exercise is to shift your focus off of your problems onto the promises of God. We are to have the mind of Christ. The scriptures help you to mature in the ways of God when you read and apply them with faith to your life. Gradually, you will bear the fruit of the Holy Spirit. God gives you everything you need to live the Christian life the minute you make Jesus your Lord and Savior. It is your responsibility to activate and develop the gifts He deposits in you.

The question I should ask is, Do you believe in Jesus? To receive deliverance, healing, or a miracle, you have to believe in the person who can do all of these things. Sometimes, He will do what He wants to show you that He loves you regardless of what you do. Jesus has no respect of person. Romans 10:9 states that "if you confess with your mouth the Lord Jesus and believe in your heart that God has raised Him from the dead, you will be saved" (NKJV). If the Lord is not your personal savior, please say the following prayer:

Lord Jesus, come into my life, forgive me of all my sins.
Please cleanse me from all unrighteousness.
Be my Lord and my personal savior,
In Jesus's name I pray, Amen.

You want to abide in Jesus and His Word to abide in you (John 15:7). One of the poems describes the fruit of the Spirit. There are nine of them in all, but let us use love and joy as an example. Personalize the scriptures below to make confessions. Confession 1 is the beginning stage of learning how to get to know Jesus. Confession 2 is the advancing stage of being thankful when you apply the scripture. You now have the confidence to tell others about your experience with Jesus out of adoration. Let us look at the first scripture.

Scripture 1: John 13:34 ~ A new commandment I give unto you, that ye love one another; as I have loved you, that ye also love one another.

Confession 1: Lord, help me to love others as You have loved me.
Confession 2: Thank You, Lord that I love others as You have loved me.

Scripture 2: Nehemiah 8:10 ~ For the joy of the Lord is your strength.

Confession 1: Lord, Your joy is my strength.
Confession 2: Thank You, Lord that Your joy is my strength.

Scripture 3: John 16:33 ~ These things I have spoken unto you, that in Me ye might have peace. In the world ye shall have tribulation: but be of good cheer; I have overcome the world.

Confession 1: Help me, Lord to have peace and be of good cheer to overcome the world.
Confession 2: Thank You, Lord for peace and that I am cheerful in overcoming this world.

Read the scriptures more than once and allow the Holy Spirit to minister to you. Write your thoughts and any revelations down in the "Your Thoughts" section provided after the "Scriptures to Ponder" section of each poem. You can make these confessions regularly or whenever you need to do so. The key is to remove anything that is negative (the problem) and replace it with something positive (the promise). The exercises are to help you renew your mind to God's way. It is a process, so evaluate yourself, notice the transformation, and celebrate what God is doing in your life. Please share your progress with everyone, including me.

No Longer Bound

Therefore if any man be in Christ, he is a new creature: old things are passed away; behold, all things are become new.
2 Corinthians 5:17

OUT WITH THE OLD YOU, IN WITH THE NEW YOU!

Please refer back to this guide if necessary.

APPENDIX 2

The Deliverance Prayer

Heavenly Father, I come before You on bended knees as Your child with praise and thanksgiving, knowing that You will do what I ask in the name of Your Son, Jesus Christ. Holy Spirit, I pray that You will quicken me to hear the voice of God and lead me in prayer. I plead the blood of Jesus in the atmosphere. Oh God, I ask that You release Your warring angels to shield me from all evil that tries to attack me or hinder me while I am in prayer with You. I walk in faith with the hope for wholeness and restoration in my spirit, in my soul, in my body, in my finances, and in my relationships. Lord, You are the way, the truth, and the life; no man comes unto our Father, but by You (John 14:6).

I take my rightful authority as a believer of Jesus Christ and use His power to tread on serpents, scorpions, and all the power of the enemy knowing that nothing shall harm me (Luke 10:19). I bind every principality, power, ruler of darkness, and spiritual wickedness in high places. According to 2 Corinthians 10:4-5, the weapons of our warfare are not carnal, but mighty through You, oh God, to the pulling down of strongholds. I cast down imaginations and every high thing that exalts itself against the knowledge of God. I bring into captivity every thought to the obedience of Christ Jesus. I put on the whole armor of God to be able to withstand the evil days. When I have done all, I will stand (Eph. 6:13). I reject every kind of evil in this world pertaining to the lust of the flesh, the lust of the eyes, and the pride of life in the name of Jesus. No longer am I ignorant of your devices, Satan, for you come to steal, kill, and destroy whether through familiar spirits, witchcraft, marine power, spirit spouses, the occult, voodoo, hoodoo, vexes, and hexes. I expose all demonic forces and spirits as weakened, defeated enemies of Jesus and I sever them with the consuming fire of the Holy Ghost. I revoke any wicked orders given to them as they relate to my life and the lives of others connected to me. Jesus, if You have made us free, we are free indeed (John 8:36).

I bind my mind to the mind of Christ. Please help me to not be conformed to this world but be transformed by the renewing of my mind so I will be able to prove what is that good, acceptable, and perfect will of God (Romans 12:2). Lord, render Your peace unto me as I keep my mind on You (Is. 26:3) and that I set my affection on the things above, not on earthly things (Col. 3:2). Let me meditate on Your precepts, and have respect for Your ways (Psalms 119:15). Lead us not into temptation, but deliver us from evil. For we are all tempted to do acts that displease You, God, but You are "faithful, who will not suffer us to be tempted above that we are able; but will with the temptation also make a way to escape, that we may be able to bear it" (1 Cor. 10:13). Lord, You were wounded for our transgressions, You were bruised for our iniquities, the chastisement of our peace was upon You, and with Your stripes we are healed (Isa. 53:5). I receive divine healing of every sickness and disease from the top of my head to the soles of my feet right now in the name of Jesus.

Lord, please supply all my needs according to Your riches in glory by Christ Jesus (Phil. 4:19). I will look to You, my help in every storm (Ps. 121:1). I stand on Your promise that You will bless what I set my hands to do as long as it is according to Your will. Let me honor You, Lord, with my substance, and with the firstfruits of all my increase (Prov. 3:9). I know that when I give, it shall be given back to me, good measure, pressed down, shaken together, and running over, men shall give me also (Luke 6:38). Lord, I thank You for giving me the power to get wealth and the wisdom to manage my finances. I am the head, not the tail; a lender, not a borrower; and above, not beneath. Satan, take your hands off of everything that belongs to me right now in the name of Jesus.

Lord, help me to confess my faults to those who come against me and learn how to pray for others since the effectual fervent prayer of a righteous man avails much (James 5:16). I am the righteousness of You, oh God. You are faithful and just to forgive me of my sins, and to cleanse me from all unrighteousness (1 John 1:9). I break every ungodly soul tie, unrighteous agreement, or word curse spoken over me, my children, my family members, and anyone connected to me, in the name of Jesus. I cut all bonds of relationships not of You, Lord, back to the beginning of time. I break every ungodly covenant made by my ancestors and break every generational curse in my bloodline at the roots with the consuming fire of the Holy Ghost, in the name of Jesus. May all bitterness, wrath, anger, clamor, and evil speaking be put away from us with all malice, and may we be kind, tenderhearted, forgiving one another, as God for Christ's sake has forgiven us (Eph. 4:31-32). I ask that You release the fullness of Your Holy Spirit to flood the places vacated by the darkness in our minds, bodies, and souls. Please fill us with Your perfect and unfailing love to have acceptance of ourselves and others, Your joy that no one can take away, Your peace that passes all understanding, Your truth that sets us free, Your dunamis power, Your humility, and all the rest of the fruit of the Spirit. Bless us, oh God, with Your faithfulness, wholeness, wellness, and with a sound mind. Free us from all fear, guilt, shame, and all addictions. May we rest in the finished works of Jesus by receiving His peace, healing, forgiveness, salvation, prosperity, and dominion. I rest in You for I am sold out to You, Lord.

Thank You, Lord that You will awaken our sleeping spirits, and bring us into the light. Thank You Lord that You will transform us as we renew our minds daily in Christ Jesus. Thank You that You will pour out Your Spirit on us, and reveal Your Word to us. Thank you, Lord, that You will give Your angels charge over us in all our ways. Jesus, I am glad that I abide in You as well as You abide in me. I will bear much fruit because You are with me (John 15:5). Since Your Word also abides in me, I believe and receive everything I have prayed for knowing that it is already done. You accepted me when I was rejected; You loved me when others hated me. You helped me when others left me for dead; You strengthened me when I was weak. You gave me joy when I was sad; You gave me wisdom when I was ignorant. You gave me truth when I was deceived; You were there with me when I was alone. You gave me peace when I was amongst confusion; You opened my spiritual eyes when I was blind. Thank You, Lord God. Thank You, Jesus. Thank You, thank You, thank You. I believe in You and may others do the same. From our innermost beings shall flow rivers of living waters. God, You have made known to me the mystery of the Gentiles, of which class I belong to. I carry the hope of glory inside of me, Your Son, Jesus. Thank You, Lord, that You will direct our hearts into the love of God as we grow in the image of Jesus Christ. In the name of Jesus I pray with thanksgiving. Amen.

FROM THE HEART:

In Colossians 1, Paul explained his true purpose of equipping the Christians to come to maturity in Christ. Yes, he suffered, yet he completed his mission as Jesus did. We, the believers of Jesus, have to grow up, reach, and teach the gospel to our generation and be disciples like those of the Bible. I like verse 28 in the Amplified Bible:

Him we preach and proclaim, warning and admonishing everyone and instructing everyone in all wisdom (comprehensive insight into the ways and purposes of God), that we may present every person mature (full-grown, fully initiated, complete, and perfect) in Christ (the Anointed One).

APPENDIX 3

Confessions of Gratitude

We should always thank God for who He is and not just for the things He does for us. Below are scriptures that I have personalized to show gratitude as if God has already done what I have asked Him for. The motive is not just to think of yourselves but others also. "Let each of you look out not only for his own interests, but also for the interests of others" (Phil. 2:4 NKJV).

Confess out loud:

Lord, I thank You that we receive one another, as Christ also received us to Your glory (Romans 15:7).

All that You give Jesus shall come to Him; and whomever that comes to Jesus, He will in no wise cast out (John 6:37).

I thank You that we stand fast in the liberty in which Christ has made us free, and we will not be entangled again with the yoke of bondage (Galatians 5:1).

We now know the truth, and the truth shall make us free (John 8:32).

Thank You for sanctifying us through Your truth for Your word is truth (John 17:17).

Dedra Johnson

Oh God, You are a Spirit: and they that worship You must worship You in spirit and in truth (John 4:24).

Let us be swift to hear, slow to speak, slow to wrath (James 1:19).

Lord, You left Your peace with us, your peace You give unto us: not as the world gives it, so let not our hearts be troubled, neither let it be afraid (John 14:27).

And we know that all things work together for good to them that love You God, to them who are called according to Your purpose (Romans 8:28).

I thank You that all our things are done with charity (1 Cor. 16:14).

There is no fear in love; but perfect love casts out fear which has torment (1 John 4:18).

We are Your Beloved, let us love one another: for love is of God; and every one that loves is born of God, and knows God (1 John 4:7).

Lord, this is the day which You have made; we will rejoice and be glad in it (Psalms 118:24).

In every thing we give thanks: for this is Your will in Christ Jesus concerning us (1 Thessalonians 5:18).

Thank You, Lord, that Your peace rules in our hearts, to which also we are called in one body; and we are thankful (Colossians 3:15).

We cast all of our care upon You, Jesus for You care for us (1 Peter 5:7).

God, You loved us so, that You gave Your only begotten Son, that whosoever believes in Him should not perish, but have everlasting life (John 3:16).

Because we know Your name, we put our trust in You: for You will not forsake those that seek You (Psalms 9:10).

For if we think we are something, when we are nothing, we deceive ourselves (Galatians 6:3).

Let nothing be done through strife or vainglory; but in lowliness of mind let us esteem each other better than ourselves (Philippians 2:3).

I thank You, Lord that we are of the same mind toward each other, that we mind not high things, but condescend of low estate. We are not wise in our own conceits (Romans 12:16).

Thank You for giving us all the things we ask for in prayer because we believe (Matthew 21:22).

For with You, God, nothing is impossible (Luke 1:37).

Thank You that our faith does not stand in the wisdom of men, but in Your power (1 Corinthians 2:5).

You are righteous, we know that every one that does righteousness is born of You (1 John 2:29).

We will flee from our youthful lusts to follow righteousness, faith, charity, peace, with them that call on You, Lord out of a pure heart (2 Timothy 2:22).

I thank You that we walk in the Spirit, so we shall not fulfil the lust of our flesh (Galatians 5:16).

As your Beloved, we will not believe every spirit, but we will try the spirits whether they are of You, God: because many false prophets are gone out into the world (1 John 4:1).

Let the Spirit of truth come and guide us into all truth: for he shall not speak of himself; but whatsoever he shall hear, that shall he speak: and he will show us things to come (John 16:13).

APPENDIX 4

Three-Part Being of Man

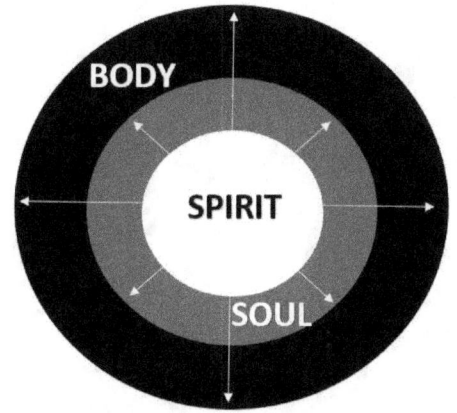

Quick Lesson

You are a spirit that possesses a soul that lives in a body. When you are born again and you have made Jesus the Lord over your life, your spirit man is filled completely with the Holy Spirit. Your soul consists of your will, mind, and emotions. The outer man is your body which includes your brain, nerves, organs, cells, and five senses (sight, hear, smell, taste, and touch). Each part of your body should align with the will of God. What is inside of you will always flow outward. If your spirit and soul are in line with God's will, your body has no other choice but to get in line.

APPENDIX 5

The Process to Destiny

There is a process that you have to go through to reach your destiny. Do you know why you are here or why you were created? You can save time and money if you do. I had no clue at first. I changed my focus to make heaven my eternal destination so my thoughts, emotions, decisions, actions, habits, and character would agree with God's Word.[1] In the example below, I used several scriptures to show the guidelines a believer of Jesus Christ would follow to pursue his or her destiny:

1. Focus: To do what pleases God (Col. 3:23, Rom. 12:12).
2. Thoughts: To think on the things above, having the mind of Christ (Phil. 2:5, 4:8).
3. Emotions: To have peace and joy (Rom. 12:18, Jam. 1:2).
4. Decisions: To trust God in all things through faith (Luke 1:37, Prov. 3:5-6).
5. Actions: Walk in love, pray, and study the Bible (1 Cor. 16:14, 2 Tim. 2:15).
6. Habits: Serve others and win souls to Christ (Rom. 12:13, Prov. 11:30).
7. Character: Godliness, hearer and doer of the Word (1 Tim. 6:6, Jam. 1:25).
8. Destination: Heaven (John 3:15, Titus 3:7).

---

1 Creflo Dollar, "Taking Authority Over Your Emotions," September 12, 2018, https://www.creflodollarministries.org/Bible-Study/Study-Notes/Taking-Authority-over-Your-Emotions

You will encounter adversity on your way to destiny. However, God is there to strengthen you when you get weary and want to give up. "Being confident of this very thing, that he which hath begun a good work in you will perform it until the day of Jesus Christ" (Phil. 1:6). Since I have a heart to save lost souls, I looked at the scriptures closely to learn how to equip the unbeliever with the right knowledge so he or she will not perish. We are living in the last days before Christ's return. I want to make sure I have dotted all i's and crossed all t's.

Galatians 5:19-21 and 1 Corinthians 6:9-10 tell us who will not inherit the kingdom of God and 2 Timothy 3:2-5 tells you who to turn away from. In your spare time, please read these scriptures. If you know you are doing one or more of the works of the flesh listed, please repent unto God. He already knows your struggles, He wants you to surrender to Him. The time is now to be obedient. Yes, we are under grace, but we should not continue in our sins. There should be a difference, a true change evident of your conversion. "And such were some of you: but ye are washed, but ye are sanctified, but ye are justified in the name of the Lord Jesus, and by the Spirit of our God" (1 Cor. 6:11). We are the righteousness of God. How can we be effective in saving the lost when we are lost, making the Word of God of no effect with our traditions? Once you know your purpose, let no one or nothing cause you to get off track. You can use this format for any focal point you may have in your life.

We can be the change we wish to see in the world if we pull together!

www.ingramcontent.com/pod-product-compliance
Lightning Source LLC
Chambersburg PA
CBHW071505070526
44578CB00001B/452